DATE DUE

About this book

Today it is very easy for you to hop on a bus to school, ride in a car on a family outing or cycle to see a friend. But many years ago, in the days of rough roads and robbers, travelling was a dangerous adventure. From those early Anglo-Saxon times to the present day, people have been discovering safer and more comfortable ways to get from one place to another.

The pictures in this book show you how roads and transport have developed, from muddy tracks to superfast motorways. You can see how the first real roads were built, how the wheel was invented and how the first letters were delivered. You can also see how your ancestors took their vegetables to market, and how *their* ancestors travelled, sword in hand, to fight the Roman invaders.

When was the first system of public transport? Earlier than you think! How did the Victorians travel to work? Why do we drive on the left? What is a *charabanc*? All your questions are answered in this exciting Eyewitness book about road transport.

Some of the words printed in *italics* may be new to you. You can look them up in the word list on page 92.

AN EYEWITNESS BOOK

Road Transport

SUSAN GOLDBLATT

WAYLAND PUBLISHERS LIMITED

More Eyewitness Books

The Railway Builders   Alistair Barrie
Pirates and Buccaneers   Tilla Brading
The Mayflower Pilgrims   Brenda Colloms
The Age of Drake   Leonard Cowie
Children of the Industrial Revolution   Penelope Davies
Country Life in the Middle Ages   Penelope Davies
Growing Up in the Middle Ages   Penelope Davies
Town Life in the Middle Ages   Penelope Davies
Canals   Jane Dorner
Markets and Fairs   Jane Dorner
Newgate to Tyburn   Jane Dorner
Kitchens and Cooking   Kathy & Mike Eldon
The Story of the Cinema   Helen du Feu
The Story of the Wheel   Peter Hames
Men in the Air   Roger Hart
The Voyages of Captain Cook   Roger Hart
Popular Entertainment   Elizabeth Holt
A Victorian Sunday   Jill Hughes
Livingstone in Africa   Denis Judd
Stagecoach and Highwayman   Stephanie McKnight
The Tudor Family   Ann Mitchell
The Horseless Carriage   Lord Montagu
The Firefighters   Anne Mountfield
The Slave Trade   Anne Mountfield
Clothes in History   Angela Schofield
Florence Nightingale   Philippa Stewart
Shakespeare and his Theatre   Philippa Stewart
Sport Through the Ages   Peter Wilson
The Glorious Age of Charles II   Helen Wodzicka
The Printer and his Craft   Helen Wodzicka
Ships and Seafarers   Helen Wodzicka

Frontispiece: A *Punch* cartoon of 1909

SBN 85340 444 5
Copyright © 1976 by Wayland (Publishers) Ltd,
49 Lansdowne Place, Hove, East Sussex
Text set in 14 pt. Photon Univers, printed by photolithography,
and bound in Great Britain at The Pitman Press, Bath

Contents

1 Dirt Track to Busy Highway   7

2 Turnpike and Stagecoach   23

3 Better Roads and Smoother Rides   37

4 Faster and Further   55

5 The World on Wheels   71

New Words   92

Table of Dates   93

More Books   94

Index   95

1. Dirt Track to Busy Highway

In Prehistoric times the only roads were tracks made by animals. These were used by men when they were out hunting. Gradually men settled in houses and villages and started farming. They travelled to neighbouring villages to trade crops for flints or furs. The pathways they made travelling to and fro had a name in Old English—*rad*. This is where our word "road" comes from.

The Romans were the first road builders in Britain. They ruled the island for 350 years, in which time they built a network of roads across England. The Roman language was Latin, and the word "transport" comes from two Latin words: *trans*, meaning "across" and *portare*, meaning "carry"—hence "to carry across". When the Romans left Britain the roads became worn and broken, because no-one knew how to repair them. In Medieval times it was thought that if you left roads alone for a while they would mend themselves. When roads were very bad, people walked on either side of them. This helped widen the roads, but often it meant that more land was churned up until it was difficult to see where the original road had been. Sometimes roads disappeared altogether.

By the Middle Ages people were regularly using carts to transport goods, but no man would ride in one alone. That was how people (like the poor man in the picture) were taken to be executed.

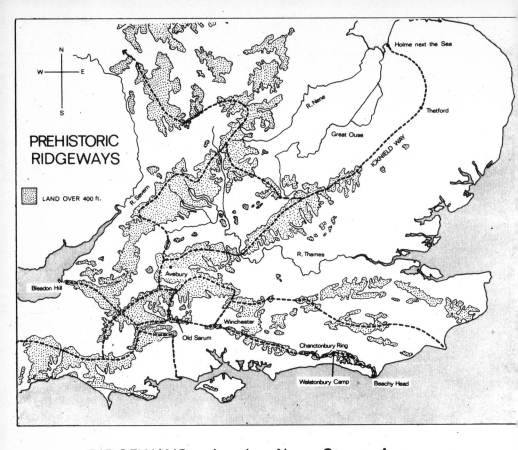

PREHISTORIC
RIDGEWAYS

LAND OVER 400 ft.

Holme next the Sea

Thetford

R. Nene

Great Ouse

ICKNIELD WAY

R. Severn

R. Thames

Avebury

Bleadon Hill

Winchester

Old Sarum

Chanctonbury Ring

Wolstonbury Camp

Beachy Head

RIDGEWAYS. In the New Stone Age, men crossed the English channel from Europe to South-East England. Most of the early trails they made led from there to Salisbury Plain, which was the richest part of the country at that time. It was probably also the religious centre. These early tracks were called "ridgeways", because they followed the hilltops, or ridges, which avoided the marshy valleys. Travellers walking along the top of a hill could also keep a lookout for robbers.

EARLY ROADS AND BRIDGES. From the Bronze Age onwards new roads were made by traders travelling between the farming villages. The people were peaceful, but robbers made travelling dangerous, so forts were built for protection about every twelve miles. That was a day's journey in those times.

8

The word "journey" means "the distance travelled in one day".

When they came to a river or stream, travellers used *fords* or tree trunks which had conveniently fallen across the water. The first man-made bridges were large boulders with flat stones laid on top.

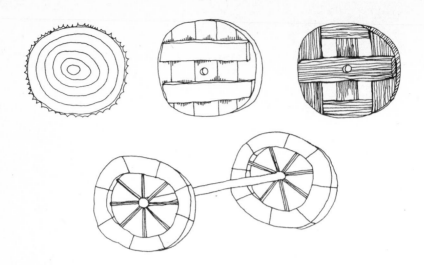

THE WHEEL.   More than three thousand years ago someone made a brilliant invention—the wheel. The first wheels were cross-sections of tree trunks. Then people made lighter wheels by joining pieces of wood together in a circle, leaving a hole in the middle. They learned how to make spokes, which strengthened the wheel without making it too heavy. Wheels were then attached to a fixed bar called an *axle* and clumsy carts were balanced on top. Before carts were invented, people had had to travel on horseback, or walk. Now several people could travel together and carry goods at the same time.

THE ROMAN INVASION.   Julius Caesar, the Roman Emperor, first landed in Britain with his troops in 55 BC, but the Roman Invasion did not take place until 43 AD. The Romans needed good roads so that they could move supplies and troops quickly to control the native Celtic people. The Romans were expert builders and their roads are still famous for their straightness. Some of the names of the Roman roads (Fosse Way, Ermine Street, Watling Street) are still used today because our modern highways follow the old roads.

11

THE CHARIOT. When they attacked Julius Caesar's invading army, the Ancient Britons rode in chariots. These were made of wickerwork covered in animal skins. By the time the Romans came to Britain they used chariots only in processions and for racing, which was a popular form of entertainment. It was a very dangerous sport. The chariots went very fast and often overturned, crushing their drivers underneath.

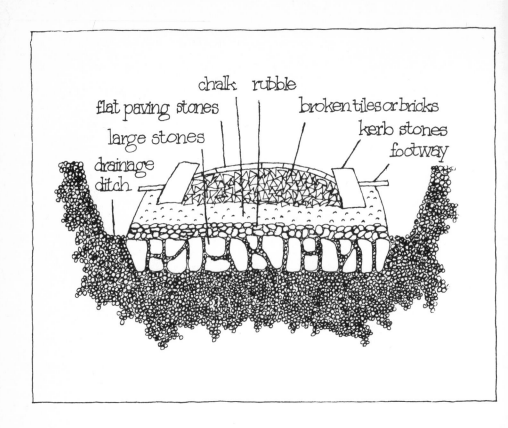

chalk rubble
flat paving stones
large stones
broken tiles or bricks
kerb stones
footway
drainage ditch

ROMAN ROADS. Roman roads were wide enough for two *legions* of soldiers marching six abreast to pass each other. Soldiers and slaves built them by digging a trench into which they put a layer of large stones. Over this were laid several layers of rubble, chalk and broken tiles. The surface was made of stone slabs cemented together and covered with gravel. The roads lasted for centuries, partly because they were so well drained. The centre was raised to form a *camber*, and small ditches on either side helped to drain the ground.

ROMAN VEHICLES. Four-wheeled carts were banned from entering towns because they were so heavy and awkward. They were difficult to turn and were useful only for carrying heavy loads on long straight roads. The two-wheeled cart was much more popular. It turned easily because the wheels were on a *pivot*. It often had a "tilt" or *awning* to protect passengers and goods from the weather. A litter, or *lectica* as the Romans called it, was a sort of sedan chair carried by slaves. Young men were ashamed to ride in them and they were used only by rich ladies or elderly officials.

15

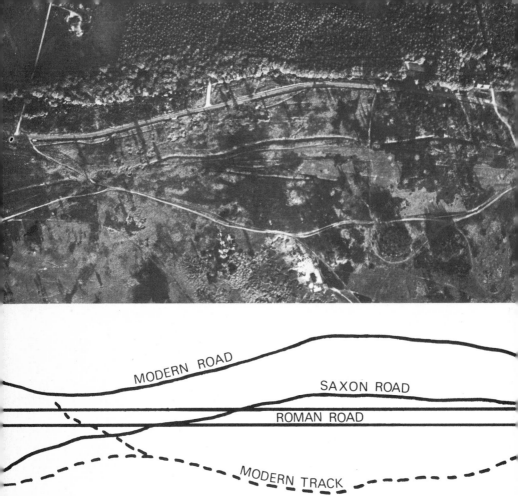

THE DARK AGES. The period after the Romans left Britain is known as the Dark Ages. Invading Saxons from the continent plundered the towns and settled in new villages in the valleys. As they travelled between villages they made new roads which were narrow and winding to avoid the woods and swamps. In the aerial photograph you can see how straight the Roman road is compared to the Saxon road which crosses it. The Saxon road is worn six feet deep in places by all the pack-horses that used it.

MEDIEVAL WAYFARERS. In the Middle Ages most people stayed in one village all their lives. Some people, however, lived on the road. They were pedlars, minstrels, friars, quack-doctors or professional pilgrims who spent their lives visiting shrines. The road between Winchester and Canterbury was so well used by pilgrims that it became known as "Pilgrims' Way". Official messengers had right of way over other traffic because they had to travel so fast. Sometimes there would be a "Royal Progress", when the King moved his whole court from one castle to another.

parle comment charlet ainsne filz
...han qui trespassa en engleterre fu
et enonie en Roy de france en leglz...
.... Et aussi fut la Royne sa femm...

MEDIEVAL TRANSPORT. Most people in Medieval times travelled on horseback. Before 1380, when the side-saddle was invented, ladies rode astride a special *pillion* seat behind a servant. Goods, especially wool, were carried by "trains" or *drifts* of up to fifty pack-horses, led by a horse wearing a bell. There were a few vehicles too. The beautiful but cumbersome "char" was used to carry court ladies and their luggage. Ladies also travelled in horse-litters which had curtains for privacy and warmth. The dying Edward I was carried in a litter at the head of his army when he invaded Scotland.

MONKS AND MONASTERIES. Monks were a great help to Medieval travellers. They collected *alms* at wayside shrines to pay for repairs to local roads. Sometimes they used the money to build a new road. Although highways were supposed to be wide enough for sixteen horsemen to ride abreast, there was very little official control, and sometimes monks acted as guides where the roads were very bad. Travellers could also take shelter in monasteries, since there were no inns where people could stay the night until the fourteenth century.

ROBBERS AND OUTLAWS.   Travelling in the Middle Ages was dangerous. There were always robbers about, who were mainly outlaws or soldiers back from the French wars. In 1285 a law called the "Statute of Winchester" said landowners had to improve roads so that "there be neither dyke nor bush, whereby a man might lurk to do hurt, within two hundred feet of the one side, and two hundred feet of the other. . ." (two hundred feet was the length of a bowshot). Unfortunately the law was not always obeyed.

2. Turnpike and Stagecoach

By Tudor times roads were in a very bad condition. People did not take much care of them and no-one knew how to repair them. Farmers would move their fences onto the roads to give themselves more land to grow crops. One farmer in Kent ploughed right across the highway and planted wheat on it. Other people took clay and stones from the roads for building.

Arthur Young, a man who travelled widely studying farming, measured the ruts in the road on a wet summer's day and had this to say: "four feet deep, and floating with mud . . . what, therefore, must it be after a winter? The only mending it receives is tumbling in some loose stones . . ."

Yet this was at a time when trade was increasing to such an extent that Henry VII was known as "the merchant Prince". This was just when people needed good roads to be able to transport goods efficiently for trade with other parts of the country and the continent.

Oxen had to drag very heavy loads, especially large pieces of timber for shipbuilding, and this was slow going. The author Daniel Defoe once described how twenty-two oxen took two years to drag one piece of timber to the coast.

Travelling was not much fun for people either. A man named John Leland said in his book *Itinerary* that people who had to travel found coaches "very noisome and tedious to travel in". ("Noisome" means smelly.)

TUDOR ROADS. After Henry VIII closed the monasteries, new laws had to be made to preserve the highways. The first Highways Act was passed in 1555. It said that each parish was responsible for the upkeep of its own roads. Later "Statute Labour" was introduced. This meant that every labourer had to repair roads for six days a year. This work was unpaid, and not very popular. Town roads were narrow, dirty and unhealthy. Houses jutted into the streets, and a man in Wells (Somerset) actually built a cookshop in the middle of the road!

TUDOR VEHICLES.   The litter was still fashionable in Tudor times. Two of the six wives of Henry VIII rode to their coronation in a horse-litter. Coaches (named after the Hungarian town Kocs where they were first made) were used in France and Holland for several years before they appeared in England. The first coach in England belonged to Mary Tudor, and Elizabeth I ordered a state coach to be built in 1564. It was very uncomfortable and the queen complained of her bruises. She preferred to ride on horseback until she arrived at the town she was visiting.

THE STAGE-WAGON. The stage-wagon, known as the "stager" or "common stage", was a big clumsy wagon pulled by eight or ten horses. It could cover about twelve miles a day. It was the first regular service between towns for goods and passengers, and cost $\frac{1}{2}$d a mile. Passengers elected a leader called the *fugleman* who arranged meals and accommodation. The "jolly waggoner", as the driver was known, walked at the head of his team of horses. He was forbidden by law to drive from the wagon in case he fell asleep.

STUART STAGE-COACHES.   Stage-coaches were
an improvement on the stage-wagon, although they
were more expensive. They stopped about every ten
or fifteen miles at an inn or "stage" to change horses
and pick up passengers. This is how they got their
name. The journey from London to York took six days
and cost £2; London to Bath took three days, and
London to Exeter five days. The stage-coach carried
six passengers inside with one or two on the roof.
Poorer passengers could travel with the luggage at
the back in a big basket called a "rumble-tumble".

INNS. By Stuart times inns were quite comfortable. They had separate rooms, whereas in Medieval times Chaucer described in his book *The Canterbury Tales* how the guests at the Tabard Inn had to share a common dormitory. Inns were very expensive, but landlords took care of their guests, and the hostess and maids welcomed travellers with a kiss. Inns had names like "The Golden Fleece" and "The Woolpack" which reflected the flourishing wool trade. Others were named after the arms of local important families, e.g. "The Red Lion" and "The White Hart".

THE POST. Cardinal Wolsey appointed the first Master of Posts to organize halts or "posts" on main roads where royal messengers could get fresh horses. Ordinary people began sending letters via the innkeepers or "postmasters". Elizabeth I and James I stopped the public post to foil spies and traitors, but Charles II encouraged it and charged 2d per sheet of letter. There were no envelopes in those days; letters were folded and sealed with a blob of wax. Postboys collected and delivered mail at post-houses, but they were often lazy and dishonest, so the service was unreliable.

HIGHWAYMEN. Slow stage-coaches were a popular target for a robber on horseback, who would stop them at a lonely spot and threaten the passengers with a pistol. These robbers were known as "highwaymen" or *tobymen* and were often admired in their neighbourhood. They worked alone, although they were often in league with innkeepers who would tell them when a very rich traveller was passing through. Noblemen travelled with guards and armed servants for protection.

BAD ROADS. Highwaymen were not the only danger for travellers. The increase of wheeled traffic on the unpaved roads was turning them into *quagmires*. The sheep, cattle and pigs which were driven to London and other big cities to feed the inhabitants did not improve the roads either. Coaches were always in danger of overturning on the bad roads or being washed away as they crossed fords. The road leading from Holyhead to Ireland was so bad in parts that coaches had to be taken to pieces and carried by sturdy Welsh peasants.

TURNPIKES. In the seventeenth century Charles II allowed trusts to be set up which arranged to collect money from people who used the roads. This money was called a toll. The toll money paid for road repairs, and the stretch of road managed by a trust was called a turnpike. Not all trusts were honest, so roads did not always improve greatly. The picture shows the famous highwayman Dick Turpin jumping a toll-gate to escape his pursuers.

TOLLGATES. The man who collected the toll money from people using his stretch of road was known as the toll-keeper. His house was six-sided so that he could see travellers approaching from all directions. Tolls varied, but on average a horse was charged 1d, a coach 4d and a wagon 6d because it did most damage to the road. *Pedestrians*, soldiers and funerals were allowed to use the road free. The picture shows some of the tickets that were issued.

Cuckoo Gate Return Ticket
Frees Aston Gate and Side Bars.

1315   185

	s.	d.
Carriage or Gig		
Waggon or Cart		
Saddle Horse		3
Cattle		
Sheep or Pigs		
Dogs or Goats		

Edgbaston Gate,

Frees Selly Oak Gate
AND BARS.

No.

Horses drawing ....
Horses not drawing ....
Beasts ....
Sheep, Calves, Pigs..

4½

20 day of Feby 1854.

Produce the Ticket or pay the Toll.

Edgbaston Gate,

Frees Selly Oak Gate and
Bars.

No.

Horses drawing ....
Saddle Horse .....
Beasts ....
Sheep, Calves, Pigs..

4½

23 day of Feb 1854.

Produce the Ticket or pay the Toll.

TOLLS

HACKNEY CARRIAGES. The first hackney carriages were the whirlicotes used in the time of Elizabeth I. In French *haquenée* means a common ambling nag, and since hackney carriages were pulled by a poor quality horse, the word was very suitable. Hackney carriages were hired for short journeys in town just as we use taxis today. They cost 1/- a mile, which was very expensive in those days. Even so they were very popular in Stuart times, when they were known affectionately as "growlers", because of the noise they made.

THE SEDAN CHAIR.   Ladies and gentlemen often rode in sedan chairs carried by two strong men. The sedan took up less room and was more comfortable than a hackney carriage, as long as the men kept in step. They could be hired at any time of the day or night, and passengers were put down outside their host's door. In rainy weather they were carried right into the hall. Wealthy families had a private sedan with the family crest on the door. The man in this picture by the famous artist Hogarth is being arrested for debt as he gets out of his sedan.

3. Better Roads and Smoother Rides

In the first half of the eighteenth century the roads were very busy. Trade was expanding and people travelled more for pleasure, but the increased traffic meant that the condition of roads grew worse. Often carts would travel over open, unfenced country which was smoother and safer than the roads, where ruts could be so deep that sometimes you could only see the heads of pedestrians walking in them.

The eighteenth century, however, was also the century of road builders. Men like Blind Jack of Knaresborough, Thomas Telford and John Macadam are famous for developing the techniques which meant the start of a new system of roads for Britain—the first real attempt at road building since the Romans had left 1,300 years before. Traffic was increasing in both quantity and quality. In his famous diary, Samuel Pepys describes his delight at helping to test the new "flying chariots", as coaches were known. There was so much traffic, and coaches changed horses so frequently, that the posting-house at Hounslow (the first stopping place outside London) kept 2,500 horses.

Probably the best known vehicles on the roads were the mail-coaches. The coachman looked very dashing in his scarlet coat with its gold braid, and the armed guard used to blow on his long trumpet for the tollkeeper to open the gate. There were no newspapers, so the mail coach carried a wooden board on which important news was written.

BROADWHEEL LAWS. It was much easier to blame vehicles for bad roads than to mend them, so many laws were passed to try and protect roads. Wagons were forbidden to carry more than a ton, and they were checked on weighing machines set up

at the side of the road. In 1751 a law was passed which said that cart-wheels must be at least nine inches wide, and carts with wheels more than sixteen inches wide were excused tolls. People thought broad wheels would help roll the road flat. In fact the clumsy vehicles did more damage than ever.

THE ROAD MENDERS.   The country really needed new roads, and the Jacobite uprising of 1715 scared people into wanting better roads so that troops could be moved quickly from place to place to defend them. The English general George Wade was ordered to build new roads in Scotland. Instead of just resurfacing them, he tried to build them properly from solid foundations. Turnpike trusts in North England employed John Metcalfe to build 180 miles of road in the Pennines. He had been blind from the age of six and was known as "blind Jack of Knaresborough". He tested the roads by prodding his way with a stick.

SECTION DRAWING OF A TELFORD ROAD

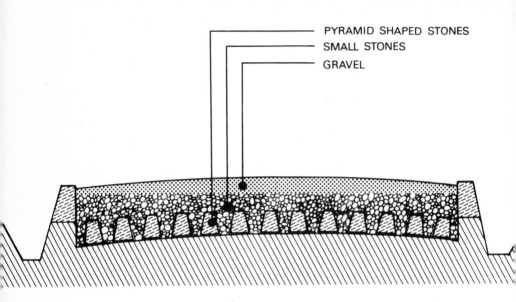

PYRAMID SHAPED STONES
SMALL STONES
GRAVEL

MACADAM ROAD

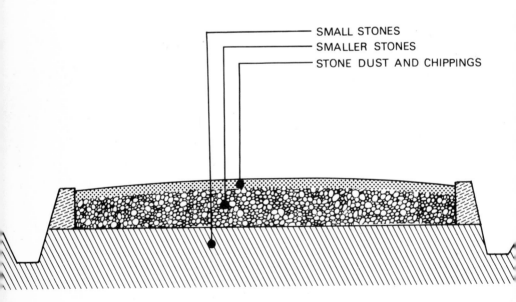

SMALL STONES
SMALLER STONES
STONE DUST AND CHIPPINGS

TELFORD AND MACADAM. Thomas Telford was chosen in 1803 to give the Scottish Highlands a proper road system. His roads were cambered for better drainage, and all the stones were carefully placed by hand. John Macadam's method was to cover old roads with layers of broken stones which became firmly locked together under the pressure of traffic. Smooth stones, which had been used before, let water through and rolled aside when coaches went over them. The "tar macadam" surface is widely used today.

GEORGIAN VEHICLES. The most common vehicles used in the Georgian countryside were clumsy wagons, made all the more ungainly by the broadwheel laws. **Carriers carts** were the poor man's alternative to the stage-wagon, and carried passengers and goods across country. The **landau** was a heavy private coach named after the German town where it was made. The upper part rolled back to make an open coach, as you can see in the picture. They were used for royal processions and state occasions almost up to the present day. A **landaulet** was similar to the landau, but lighter and more graceful.

THE POST CHAISE. The fastest means of travel in Georgian times was by post chaise. This was a light, covered carriage pulled by two or four horses. Some were privately owned, but they could be hired for 1/- a mile. At forty miles a day this was very expensive. The post chaise had no driver, but a *postilion* rode on the nearside horse. He wore a *livery* consisting of a short blue jacket, yellow waistcoat and white hat and breeches. The postilion was hired at a posting-house when the horses were changed.

STAGE-COACHES. Stage-coaches had extravagant names like *Comet, Highflyer, Reliance, Spitfire* and *Super-Safety*. The coaches looked very splendid with their coats of paint and varnish. By now outside passengers had proper seats, and windows were made of glass (instead of wooden or leather shutters). Coach journeys were advertised, and some notices said passengers were not to tip the driver and guards if they did not keep strictly to the timetable. Coaches had to travel very fast on flat ground to keep up their average speed of 12 mph.

46

CARRIAGES.　The **gig** was a two-wheeled vehicle for one or two passengers. It had many variations. A gig with a hood was called a **cabriolet**. A **curricle** was pulled by two horses, while a **sulky** only had room for the driver. A **whisky** was a light two-wheeled carriage with springs underneath long shafts. The ordinary gig hung from springs suspended on straps. The suspension of vehicles generally had improved by Georgian times, and carriages were much more comfortable. The **perch phaeton** (pronounced "fay-ton") was a smart carriage for the rich. The picture shows George IV driving a phaeton through Windsor Park.

INNS.　Inns were cheaper than the posting-houses, but travelling was still expensive, especially when you had to tip the driver sixpence at every stop as well as pay for lodgings about every thirty-five miles. Breakfast and dinner cost about half-a-crown each. Poor people had to eat in the kitchen, and "outsiders" (who sat on top of the coach) could not eat with "insiders", until young noblemen made it fashionable to ride up with the driver.

THE MAIL-COACH. Stage-coaches were not allowed to carry letters, but they were so much cheaper and more reliable than postboys that people disguised their letters as parcels and sent them by coach. In 1784 John Palmer suggested that special stage-coaches should be organized to deliver mail, and eventually the Prime Minister (then William Pitt) allowed him to start a mail-coach service. Mail coaches also carried passengers, but as you can see from the picture the journey was not always very comfortable. In 1812 two passengers froze to death in the London to Bath mail-coach.

HIGHWAYMEN. Travelling by stage-coach or mail-coach was all the more dangerous because of attacks by highwaymen. Passengers dreaded to hear the words "Your money or your life!" One of the most famous of all highwaymen was Dick Turpin. In this picture you can see him faced with the possible fate awaiting all highwaymen. Claude Duval was a highwayman well known for his gentlemanly manners, and there was even a highwaywoman. She was called Moll Cutpurse and was so ugly she used to disguise herself as a man.

THE CHARABANC. The "brake", or charabanc (pronounced "sharrerbang" in English), was the first pleasure transport to cater for poor people. It was a long horse-drawn wagon with wooden seats and open sides, and passengers had a clear view all round. It was used for cheap rides and outings, especially trips to the seaside, when it looked very gay with its striped awning to keep off the sun. The charabanc was first used in Queen Victoria's reign, and it remained popular until after the Great War of 1914—18.

THE HANSOM CAB. The hansom cab was designed by Joseph Hansom in about 1834. It was very popular because it was much lighter and quicker than the hackney carriage. The hansom had two wheels and could carry two passengers who faced forwards. The cabbie sat behind them and could speak to them through a trap-door in the roof. Since no-one has bothered to change some of the laws passed in Victorian times, a modern taxi-driver is still legally supposed to carry a bale of hay for his horse!

VICTORIAN VEHICLES. Sedan chairs had almost vanished from the streets by the time Queen Victoria came to the throne in 1837. Many more people who could afford it now owned private carriages; a carriage and pair was a sign of importance and wealth. Two recently introduced carriages were the **victoria**, named after the queen, and the **brougham** (shown in the picture). This was an aristocratic closed carriage named after the politician Lord Brougham. In the country the doctor's trap and the farmer's gig were a familiar sight, while rich children and their governess would travel in a pony cart.

4. Faster and Further

Dr Arnold, the famous headmaster of Rugby school, said that railways would mean "the end of feudality" in England. What he meant was that most people would stop earning a living by farming and working on the land, and more people would live in towns and work in factories. England was the first country in the world to have an Industrial Revolution. After this machinery was used to do jobs which had been difficult or even impossible for men to do on their own. One factory could now provide goods to sell all over the country, and trade with other countries was increasing. This meant that the country needed a better transport system.

Mechanical forms of transport were being developed, powered first by steam, then by electricity and petrol. Very early in the Industrial Revolution the scientist-poet Erasmus Darwin forecast the widespread use of mechanical transport (including aeroplanes) in a poem:

"Soon shall thy arm unconquered steam afar,
Drag the slow barge, or drive the rapid car;
Or on wide waving wings expanded bear
The flying chariot thro' the fields of air!"

Railways and canals were developed and improved quickly but mechanized road transport and roads themselves did not improve until much later. In the picture you can see a train going over a bridge while the traffic in the street below is still drawn by horses.

RIVALS (1): Railways.   The first railway was really a tramway with iron rails, used to move coal. With the invention of steam the trucks were pulled by a steam-engine and became a serious rival to road transport. Roads were inadequate for heavy traffic and in turn heavy traffic damaged the roads, so many industries transported their goods by rail. Railways were also the cheapest form of passenger transport, and although coachmen called the new steam engines "steam kettles", they were so cheap and quick that for a long time railways were more important than roads.

RIVALS (2): Canals. Canals were the other main rival of road transport. One thirty-ton barge could carry the combined load of 240 pack-horses. The Romans had built a canal in 120 AD called "Fossdyke", but the first "modern" canal in England was built by the Duke of Bridgewater in 1759. Barges used it to move coal from the Worsley coal pits to Salford and Manchester. Canals are known as the "motorways of the nineteenth century", but they are little used today except for pleasure trips.

STEAM INVENTIONS. A working steam-engine was invented more than two thousand years ago by Hero of Alexandria. In the seventeenth century a Frenchman named Denis Papin also experimented with steam. Most of his experiments blew up, but some of his ideas were used by Thomas Newcomen, who built a steam-engine which pumped water out of mines. This in turn was improved in 1766 by James Watt, who also made other steam-driven machinery. The first steam-locomotive was built in 1804 by Richard Trevithick, and twenty-five years later Robert Stevenson built his famous *Rocket*—the father of modern steam locomotives.

STEAM-CARRIAGES. A Cornishman named Dr Gurney started the first regular steam-carriage service in 1827. His steam-coach carried eighteen passengers at ten mph. Despite heavy road tolls and competition from the railways, several other steam-coach companies were set up in the 1830s. A man named Dr Church ran a service from London to Birmingham which carried fifty passengers at the unheard of speed of twenty mph. A fleet of steam-coaches in London, run by Walter Hancock, had names like the *Enterprise*, the *Erin* and the *Autopsy*. Unfortunately the steam-coaches were always in great danger of blowing up.

THE RED FLAG ACT. As more steam-coaches took to the roads, Parliament passed laws to protect pedestrians and the road surfaces. The Act of 1865 reduced the maximum speed to four mph and said that a man carrying a red flag had to walk sixty yards in front of each vehicle to warn people of the approaching monster. Eventually in 1869 the speed limit was raised to twelve mph. The motorists celebrated with the "Old Crock's Race" from London to Brighton which is now an annual event.

THE HORSE-DRAWN BUS. The first bus was drawn by three horses, carried twenty-two people and was run in London in 1829 by a man named George Shillibeer. His "omnibus", (omnibus is a Latin word meaning "for all") ran from the City to a Public House on the Edgeware Road. Each journey cost 1/-. As more and more buses took to the road they were painted different colours. Shillibeer's bus was green with yellow wheels and red curtains. There were no fixed stopping places and there were often dangerous races for passengers, sometimes ending in fights between rival conductors.

DOUBLE-DECKERS. In 1851 so many visitors came to London for the Great Exhibition in Hyde Park that seats were put on the roofs of buses so that they could carry more people. These were the first double-deckers. They were known as "knife-board" buses because the back-to-back seats reminded the Victorians of a sort of knife-box they had at that time. The knife-board buses carried ten passengers inside and fourteen on top. Only men went onto the roof because women could not get up the narrow ladder in their long skirts.

THE HORSELESS CARRIAGE. Engineers in England were held back in their experiments by the heavy restrictions of the Red Flag Act. In France and Germany, however, they were still trying to produce a "horseless carriage" which would be safer and do less damage than the steam-coach. A German named Karl Benz built the first motor-car in 1885, using the petrol engine invented by another German, Gottlieb Daimler. The picture shows the first car built by Daimler himself.

TRAMS. The first tram service operated in Lancashire in about 1860. Originally trams were pulled along fixed rails by horses, but soon they were powered by electricity. You can still see electric trams in Blackpool, although they are not used much anywhere else now. Because they ran on tracks trams could not turn round, so they were built to be driven from both ends. To go back along his route the driver just walked to the other end of the tram. Sometimes the seat-backs were moveable so that passengers could face the other way too.

TROLLEY-BUSES. Trolley-buses gradually became more popular than trams. They could move about the road more easily than trams, which ran on fixed rails. Also trolley-buses could overtake other vehicles, although their "arms" stopped them from overtaking each other. The conductor carried a long bamboo pole to put the arms back on the electric wires when they came off, which they frequently did. Installing and repairing the electric cables for trolley-buses was very expensive, so they were only used in large towns.

THE BICYCLE. The word "bicycle" comes from the Latin word *bi* and the Greek *kyklos*, and means "two-wheeled". The Comte de Sivrac invented the first bicycle in France in 1791. The *Célérifère*, as it was called, was simply a two-wheeled hobby-horse or dandy-horse. The rider could not steer, and had to push it along with his feet. In 1871 the German Baron de Sauerbron produced his *Draisienne*. It had an armrest, and the moveable front wheel meant it could be steered. Although many people made fun of them, hobby-horses were very popular as a pastime with the nobility.

THE BONESHAKER. A Scottish blacksmith called Kirkpatrick McMillan built the first pedal-operated bicycle in 1839. The pedals drove the back wheel. In 1861, in Paris, Pierre and Ernest Michaux produced a bicycle whose pedals were fixed to the hub of the front wheel. They called their machine the "velocipede", which means "swift feet". It had no springs and was so uncomfortable that in England it was known as the "boneshaker". One of the later improvements was the cycle lamp, which was originally a candle in a small box attached to the handlebars.

'THE HOBBY HORSE DEALER.'

'THE LADY'S ACCELERATOR.'

THE PENNY-FARTHING. Since one turn of the boneshaker's pedals caused the wheel to turn once, it followed that the bigger the wheel, the greater the distance covered with each push of the pedals. The front wheel was made bigger until it was as much as five feet across, while the back wheel was only about sixteen inches in diameter. This "ordinary" bicycle, as it was called, became known from its appearance as the Penny-Farthing. It was difficult to ride (especially to start and stop), but Penny-Farthing races were held and they could travel up to 20 mph.

THE SAFETY BICYCLE. Riding a Penny-Farthing could be dangerous, so cyclists welcomed the safety bicycle, invented by T. K. Starley of Coventry. His bicycle, which he called the *Rover*, had two small wheels of about equal size. The pedals drove a gear wheel attached by a chain to the hub of the back wheel. Ladies wore special clothes for cycling, as long skirts were impractical. Mrs Amelia Bloomer designed the baggy trousers known as "bloomers". Ladies also wore the "rational costume" which consisted of a long jacket, knickerbockers, woollen stockings and a straw hat.

5. The World on Wheels

A petrol station is a fairly common sight today, but it is only in the last fifty years that motor transport has become available to everyone. At present in Britain there are fifteen million motor vehicles. This great increase in traffic meant that roads had to be improved, and the turnpike trusts could not do it alone. An Act of Parliament in 1888 made County Councils responsible for the upkeep of their own roads. Since 1919, however, although local councils pay for the upkeep of smaller roads, there has been a Ministry of Transport which organizes the road system throughout the country. The "road fund", which pays for repairs and road building, gets its money from the tax paid on petrol and on all vehicles.

When cars were first made, anyone who could afford to buy a car was allowed to drive it. Today there is much more control over road use. All vehicles must be insured and have a registration number (the one you see on the number plate). Only vehicles owned by the Queen do not have a registration number. Every driver must pass a test to get a licence to prove that he is fit to drive. There is a maximum speed limit of seventy mph throughout the country, which is reduced to thirty mph in built up areas. All cars must be fitted with seat belts, and now there is more publicity to try and make people drive more safely.

MODERN BUSES. This is an unusual view of a double-decker bus. The roll of signs has been pulled out to show the list of possible *destinations*. Until recently bus *crews* did not wear uniform. A crew normally consists of two people: a driver and a conductor. The conductor used to be nicknamed a "cad". Today we also have "pay-as-you-enter" buses, in which the driver sells the tickets.

MOTOR BUSES. Horse-drawn buses and trams had disappeared from London by 1914. Various engines were used to power buses before they finally settled on the diesel engine used today. Until 1930 the top deck of a double-decker was open, and passengers had a waterproof apron attached to the seat in front to pull over their laps when it rained. You can still sometimes see open-topped buses at the seaside.

MODERN BICYCLES.   Bicycles were first mass produced in 1914. The modern bicycle is really only an improved version of Starley's safety bicycle. The major difference is that it uses *pneumatic* tyres, invented by J. B. Dunlop in 1888. Today tricycles have almost disappeared except for use by young children, and you rarely see the tandem (two-seater). Cycling is a popular sport, however, and races are held throughout the country nearly every weekend. Most racing bikes have the dropped handlebars you can see in the picture.

COACHES.   Coaches are specially designed for long-distance travel. They go faster and have fewer stops than ordinary buses and are smoother over bumpy roads. They have air-conditioning and heaters to maintain a comfortable temperature, and fans to circulate the air because the large windows are not designed to open. The driver sits inside the coach with the passengers and has a clear view through the wide, curved windscreen. There is usually a large boot to carry all the luggage.

MOTOR-BIKES.   Adding a small petrol engine to a
bicycle was an obvious improvement which soon
became very popular. It meant less work for the rider,
and he could go much faster than on an ordinary
bicycle. There have been various designs for carrying
passengers. Today, the passenger usually sits astride
behind the driver, but there have been wickerwork
cycle-cars pulled behind the bike, "combinations" of
bike and side-car, and even motor-tricycles where
the passenger was carried in front.

THE POPULAR CAR.   Early cars were very expensive because they were all built by hand. In 1908, to save money, Henry Ford started making cars all the same style and colour. He is famous for saying: "Any customer can have a car painted any colour he wants so long as it's black." In 1912 he began mass production of his best design—the Model "T" Ford. It became very popular and was known affectionately as *Tin Lizzie*. The quick, cheap production methods meant many more people could afford cars.

RACING CARS. Racing cars, like the one in the picture, are designed to be driven especially fast. Their average speed is about 100 mph. Notice the wide wheels for stability and the roll-bar behind the driver's head to protect him if the car turns over. Racing helps car builders to discover the strongest and most reliable ways of building cars because it puts a strain on the engine and body that only the best *components* can survive.

MORE CARS. The first modern car (the 1901 Mercedes) has been the standard design for cars ever since. There are, however, many different models and makes on the roads today. Two of the more popular cars are the German-produced Volkswagen (which means "people's car") and the English "mini". They are small, easy to park, and don't use much petrol. The Volkswagen—nicknamed "the beetle" because of its shape—has its engine at the back, while the mini's engine is fitted sideways to save space.

ELECTRICAL VEHICLES.   Most vehicles today are driven by petrol or diesel engines (which run on oil), but a few are powered by electricity, which has the advantage of not polluting the atmosphere. Electrically-powered vehicles don't need overhead wires like the old trams. Their electricity is stored in batteries. They cannot travel very far or fast but they are ideal for short journeys, such as house-to-house deliveries. Most milk-floats, for example, are powered by electricity.

VEHICLES OF THE FUTURE. Dr Felix Wankel, a German engineer, has been working on a rotary piston engine since 1951. It might replace the ordinary piston engine generally used at the moment because it is quieter and gives more power for its weight. It is still fuelled by petrol, which is becoming very expensive, so other people are experimenting on electric vehicles. Electric buses are already being used in Manchester, and the picture shows an experimental electric car.

VEHICLES THAT SAVE LIVES.   The sirens and
flashing lights of fire-engines and ambulances warn
other motorists to keep out of their way. They are
probably going to save somebody's life. For this they
carry special equipment. Fire-engines are equipped
with powerful pumps which force water through the
hose-pipes at high pressure. They also carry an
extension ladder or a hydraulic-lift platform to rescue
people trapped high up in buildings. Ambulances
carry stretcher beds and other medical supplies and
equipment to care for people being taken to hospital.

COMMERCIAL VEHICLES. Vehicles used by businesses are called commercial vehicles. They are made in many shapes and sizes. Vans are used to transport small loads over short distances and lorries or trucks carry heavier goods. The picture shows vans and trucks of various sizes, although this is not a typical cargo! Real car-transporters are lorries specially designed for their load. Other specially-designed vehicles include horse and cattle boxes and tankers to carry oil or other liquids in bulk.

ARTICULATED LORRIES. "Rigid" vehicles are built all in one piece, but the picture shows an "articulated" lorry, where the cab or tractor can be separated from the semi-trailer. The tractor, the part that powers the vehicle, is a lorry without a body. It contains the engine and has the two front pairs of wheels. The trailer is attached on a pivot to make turning easier. Articulated lorries save time because cargo can be loaded or unloaded from a trailer while the tractor is transporting goods elsewhere on another trailer.

MOTORWAYS. Today's high speed traffic needs special roads. Motorways are wide and straight and have separate carriageways for vehicles travelling in opposite directions. This lessens the danger of accidents. The photograph of the junction at Gravelly Hill (known as "Spaghetti Junction", for obvious reasons) shows how complicated it can be to change direction on a motorway. The first motorway was opened in Preston in 1958, and the M1 runs between London and Birmingham.

84

CONSTRUCTION VEHICLES. Many different vehicles are involved in the construction of roads. Bulldozers knock down small buildings or trees, and the heavy rubble is carried away by dumper trucks. The huge excavators have caterpillar or crawler tracks so that they can move easily over rough ground. The truck mixer's rotating body stops the ready-mixed cement it carries from setting before it reaches its destination. Spreading machines, vibrators and steam-rollers are all used for laying the road surface.

MUNICIPAL SERVICES. *Municipal* vehicles are owned by local councils, and their job is to keep streets and homes clean and healthy. The refuse collector, or dustcart, has a ram device to compress the refuse as it is taken in. Some have special equipment for unloading waste-bins, as you can see in the picture. Other typical municipal vehicles have road-sweepers or water-sprayers attached for keeping the roads clean.

LIFE ON THE ROAD.   The people in the picture are gypsies who live in the caravan behind them. Some of the older gypsies still have horse-drawn caravans but today many buy modern caravans which are pulled by cars. Many holiday-makers also know the pleasures of living in a caravan and being able to take their home with them when they travel. Others convert buses or coaches into mobile homes.

TWENTIETH-CENTURY ROADS.   Building new roads is a complicated process nowadays. Surveyors and engineers have to map out a suitable route and then the plans are approved by local authorities. Excavators are used to remove earth, the road bed is rolled flat, and then usually it is sprayed with *bitumen* to make it waterproof. The two main kinds of road surface are *asphalt* and concrete. In the picture the machine—called a "paver"—is laying the asphalt surface of a new road.

REMNANTS OF THE PAST. Despite all the highly-mechanized transport on our roads today, there are still some reminders of the old way of life. On ceremonial occasions the queen rides in a horse-drawn carriage. Most people have seen the rag and bone man's horse and cart. The brewer's *dray* is loaded with barrels and crates and pulled by

beautiful shire horses, and in London some of the policemen are mounted. Even our custom of driving on the left is a reminder of the time when horsemen rode on the left, so that if attacked by someone coming in the opposite direction, they could defend themselves with their right hand, using a sword or a pistol.

New Words

Alms	Money given to the poor out of charity
Asphalt	A hard substance used to cover roads
Awning	A covering to shelter passengers from the weather; also called a "tilt"
Axle	A rod connecting two wheels, on which the wheels turn
Bitumen	A kind of tar used to waterproof road surfaces
Camber	The shape of the surface of a road which is higher in the middle than at the sides
Component	One of the parts of which something is made up
Crew	A team who operate a bus, train, aeroplane etc.
Destination	The place to which one is going
Dray	A strong cart for heavy goods
Drift	A group of pack-horses; also called a "train"
Ford	A place to cross a river where the water is shallow
Fugleman	The leader of a group of travellers in Medieval times
Legion	A body of Roman soldiers, three to six thousand strong
Livery	The clothes worn by a servant or tradesman
Municipal	Belonging to a local government council
Pedestrian	Someone walking or travelling on foot
Pillion	A cushion behind a horseman for a second rider

Pivot	A piece of wood or metal on which something turns
Pneumatic	Inflated with air
Postilion	A man who rides one of the horses pulling a carriage to guide them
Quagmire	An area of soft, wet, boggy ground
Tobyman	Another name for a highwayman

Table of Dates

43AD	Roman Invasion
1555	First Highways Act, introducing "Statute Labour"
1663	First turnpike trust set up on the Great North Road
1751	"Broadwheel Law" introduced
1759	Bridgewater Canal built
1784	First Mail-coach from Bath to London
1791	First bicycle, the *Célérifère*
1825	Stockton & Darlington railway opened to goods and passengers
1827	First regular steam-carriage service
1829	Robert Stevenson builds the *Rocket*
1829	Shillibeer's omnibus in service
1860	Trams in service in Lancashire
1861	The "boneshaker" invented
1865	"Red Flag Act" introduced
1885	Karl Benz's motor car built
1908	Model "T" Ford developed
1912	Mass production of Model "T" Ford begins
1958	First motorway opened in Preston

More Books

Barrie, Alistair. *The Railway Builders* (Wayland, 1973). Another book in the Wayland Eyewitness Series, describing the major rival of road transport.

Carey, David. *The Ladybird Book of Motor Cars* (Wills & Hepworth, 1968). A useful book for identifying cars on the road today.

Carter, Ernest F. *Veteran Cars* (Burke, 1959 & 1972). A complete book for the real car lover.

Kohn, Bernice. *The Look-it-up Book of Transport* (Collins, 1971). An alphabetical guide to all forms of transport all over the world.

Levinson, Maurice & Sadler, Brent. *On the Buses* (Wayland, 1973). A close look at today's buses and the people who work on them.

McKnight, Stephanie. *Stagecoach and Highwayman* (Wayland, 1973). The full background to the thrilling period of stage-coaching in Britain.

Ray, John. *Cars* (Adam & Charles Black, 1973). A general study of cars—how they are built, their history and their future.

Unstead, R. J. *Travel by Road Through the Ages* (Adam & Charles Black, 1969). An excellent book looking at road transport from Prehistoric times to the present day.

Wyatt, Robert. *Cars* (Macdonald, 1971). A thorough look at cars, including a section on car design.

Index

Ambulance, 82

Bicycles, 66, 68, 69, 75
Broadwheel laws, 38, 39
Buses, 61, 63, 72

Canals, 55, 57
Carriages, 44, 53
Cars, 63, 71, 77, 78
Carts, 7, 10, 15, 37, 43, 53
Char, 19
Charabanc, 50
Chariot, 12
Coaches, 23, 24, 31, 37, 43, 75
Commercial vehicles, 83, 84
Construction vehicles, 87, 88

Dark Ages, 16

Electrically-powered vehicles, 64, 65, 80, 81

Fire-engine, 82
Fords, 9, 31

Georgian vehicles, 43–7
Gigs, 44, 53

Hackney carriages, 34, 35, 53

Hansom cabs, 53
Highwaymen, 31, 50

Industrial Revolution, 55
Inns, 20, 27, 28, 30, 47

Laws, 21, 24, 38, 60, 71
Life on the road, 88
Litters, 15, 19, 24
Lorries, 83, 84

Macadam, John, 37, 43
Mail-coach, 37, 49, 50
Medieval times, 7, 17, 19, 28
Middle Ages, 7, 17, 19, 28
Monks and monasteries, 9, 24
Motor-bikes, 76
Motorways, 84
Municipal services, 87

Penny-Farthing, 68
Post, 44, 47
Post chaise, 44
Post-houses, 28, 44, 47

Railways, 55, 56, 59
Red Flag Act, 60, 63
Remnants of the past, 90

Ridgeways, 8
Road building and repair, 7,
    9, 14, 23, 31, 37, 40, 43,
    71, 87, 88
Robbers, 9, 21
Romans, 7, 10–16, 57

Saxons, 16
Sedans, 15, 35, 53
Stage-coaches, 24, 27, 30,
    45, 49, 50
Stage-wagons, 26, 27, 43
Steam inventions, 56, 58, 59

Stuart times, 23, 27, 28, 34

Telford, Thomas, 37, 43
Tollgates, 32, 38
Trams, 64, 65, 72
Trolley-buses, 65
Tudor times, 23, 24
Turnpikes, 32, 40, 71

Vehicles of the future, 81
Victorian vehicles, 50, 53

Wheel, 10

Picture Credits

The author and publisher would like to thank all those who have given permission for copyright pictures to be reproduced on the following pages: Mary Evans Picture Library, 9, 15, 20, 21, 22, 24, 30, 51, 66, 76; The Mansell Collection, 38/39, 40, 41; Aerofilms Limited, 16, 85; The Science Museum, London, 43, 56, 58, 59; Leicester Mercury, 45; British Waterways Board, 57; John Goldblatt Esq, 61, 62; Leicester Reference Library, 64, 65; Esso Petroleum Co Ltd, 70; London Transport Executive, 73; Raleigh Industries Ltd, 74; Duple Coachbuilders Ltd, 75; Ford Motor Co, 77, 83; Geoff Roberts Esq, 78; British Leyland, 79; Susan Goldblatt, 80, 87; Owen Rowlands Esq, 82; J. Brockhouse & Co Ltd, 84; Rubery Owen & Co Ltd, 86; Aveling-Barford Ltd, 86; Blaw Knox Ltd, 88; Irish Tourist Board, 89; Courage Ltd, 90/91.

Diagrams were kindly supplied by:
Anne Masters, 10, 11, 14; Douglas Lee Esq, 16; Lindsay Loxton, 41.
The remaining illustrations are the property of the Wayland Picture Library.